Quick Healthy Meals

A cookbook with healthy, balanced recipes that are prepared in 30 minutes or less.

By Misty Knight

READ THIS FIRST

DOWLOAD THE PDF VERSION FOR FREE!

Just to say thanks for buying my book, I would like to give you the PDF version of the book, and all the forms from the book for FREE!

Visit
www.atenaciouswoman.com/cookbook

Watch the Getting Started Video!

If you are overwhelmed, and don't know where to start, watch my introductory video. I will walk you through getting started on your health journey. I will explain how to use the meal planner and how to pick your meals for the week. Learn exactly what I did to lose 50 pounds!

Visit
www.atenaciouswoman.com/cookbook

Follow us on our social pages!

WWW.FACEBOOK.COM/ATENACIOUSWOMAN

WWW.INSTAGRAM.COM/MISTYKNIGHT777

Acknowledgements

I would like to thank my amazing husband for always encouraging me to go for my dreams, and for his never-ceasing love that melts my heart.

I would also like to thank the beautiful ladies who helped me put all this together. Brandi, Wendy, Suzan, Kat, Sarah, and Mandy, thank you for the invaluable input you provided me as I wrote this book and developed my program.

Author Biography

I have been married to the love of my life for almost one year now. We have ve beautiful children together ranging in ages from 15 to 5! They are all involved in sports and school activities, and we both work full-time outside the home. This challenge helped me to master eating healthy efficiently. I created this cookbook and my Health and Fitness Program to help other busy women like me, grow their health and fitness pillar of their lives.

I love helping people discover that they too can be healthy, and that it is a lot easier than they think! Visit my website today to learn how I help others achieve their health and fitness goals.
www.atenaciouswoman.com/cookbook

INTRODUCTION

Five years ago, I was 60 pounds overweight. I was tired all the time. I had headaches daily, and had Hashimoto's Hypothyroidism. I was miserable. I didn't want to play with my kids because was always tired. I didn't feel good about myself and none of my clothes fit.

I decided it was time to get healthy. I began a new diet and started working out. I was told to avoid processed foods, bread, and sugar because of my hypothyroidism; from research I did, I figured Paleo would be a good diet for me.

I did very well on the Paleo diet. I had energy again, my headaches were pretty much gone, and I lost about 20 pounds with the diet and exercise. I felt so much better. I had energy to play with my kids again!

I stayed on the diet and became pregnant with my second baby. I didn't gain as much weight with my second baby as I had with my first. After my baby was born, I began working out more intensely with weightlifting. I lost a total of 50 pounds after the birth of my baby. I loved my body—I felt like that sexy mom I had always wanted to be. I had tons of energy to workout, work, and play with my kids. And the best part was, my Hashimoto's disappeared! I was able to completely get off medication, which my doctors had previously told me I would be on for the rest of my life!

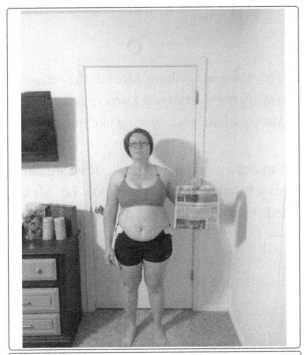

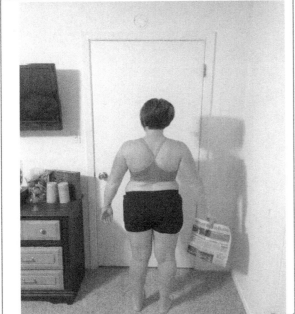
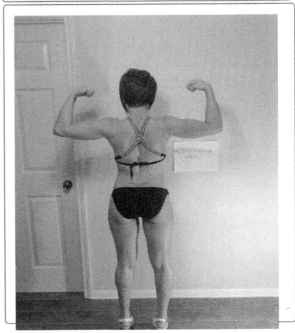

THE PROBLEM

Paleo recipes are delicious, but they tend to be very time-consuming. Most of the recipes involve chopping vegetables and using multiple pans at every meal. I felt like I was spending all my time in the kitchen. When I went back to work, I couldn't keep up with cooking like that anymore.

I adapted the recipes in this cookbook to fit into an active and busy lifestyle. They are pulled from my past four years of eating various diets, including Paleo, gluten-free, and low-fat. My goal with these recipes is to have your snacks and lunches prepped on Sundays in less than one hour, and for all your dinners to be done in 30 minutes or less.

Healthy eating should be accessible for everyone, not just the select few who have the time to cook gourmet meals!

WHAT TO BUY

Plastic Bags
You will need sandwich bags for your snacks and for steaming veggies.

Steam-able Veggie Packs
You can find these in both the fresh and frozen sections. I prefer getting the frozen veggies because they don't go bad.

Thin-sliced Chicken
The goal is to have dinners cooked in 30 minutes or less. If you buy regular chicken breasts, they will take much longer than that to cook completely. And, if you butterfly them yourself, you have an extra knife and cutting board to wash. So, I pay a little bit more for the thin-sliced chicken to save time.

Canned Chicken
I have tried many different types of chicken in my lunches, and all of them seem to have a weird flavor when I eat them. The only one I have tried that never has a weird flavor is the canned chicken. This also saves a ton of prep time. I recommend the 5 oz. cans for lunches. If you can only find the 10 oz. cans, you can use them for two meals.

Rice Cups
We will use brown rice in the lunch and dinner recipes. To save time, I recommend purchasing the brown rice cups. You just put these in the microwave for 60 seconds. This saves quite a bit of prep time and reduces dishes as well.

Minced garlic
I love the flavor of garlic in my meals, but it's time-consuming to use fresh garlic. I recommend purchasing a jar of minced garlic to easily add garlic to any meal.

Potato Bag

You can have perfectly cooked sweet potatoes in just 4 minutes with these handy little bags! They make adding a sweet potato to your meals super quick and easy. You can usually fit two potatoes in each bag. If you buy two bags, you may be able to cook four potatoes at once!

Pico de Gallo

I love spicy food. Pico gives you a good amount of spice and it's a quick and easy addition to eggs and burritos. I buy the already prepared Pico at my supermarket.

Coconut Aminos

You can find bottled coconut aminos in the same section as the apple cider vinegar. It tastes like soy sauce, but it's much healthier for you.

HOW TO USE THE COOKBOOK

You will need to pick a breakfast, lunch, dinner, and two snacks for each day. You can have a cheat day on Saturday, or three total cheat meals per week. Below is a sample meal plan that you can copy for each week.

I have intentionally portioned the recipes for just one serving (one person). This makes it easy for you to multiply the ingredients based on how many people you need to cook for. I have also included family meal tips for the dinners. My kids are picky eaters, and the tips show how I either modify the meals for the kids or what they eat instead. I know many people say to make your kids eat whatever you cook, but for me, this is one of those battles I just don't care to have. This works for us and that's what matters to me! I hope the tips will help your family as well!

Simple Healthy Meal Planner

Sunday
- Breakfast
- Snack
- Lunch
- Snack
- Dinner
- Family Notes

Monday
- Breakfast
- Snack
- Lunch
- Snack
- Dinner
- Family Notes

Tuesday
- Breakfast
- Snack
- Lunch
- Snack
- Dinner
- Family Notes

Wednesday
- Breakfast
- Snack
- Lunch
- Snack
- Dinner
- Family Notes

Thursday
- Breakfast
- Snack
- Lunch
- Snack
- Dinner
- Family Notes

Friday
- Breakfast
- Snack
- Lunch
- Snack
- Dinner
- Family Notes

Saturday
- Breakfast
- Snack
- Lunch
- Snack
- Dinner
- Family Notes

Shopping List

Produce	Dry Goods	Frozen	Meats	Dairy

SPICE BLENDS

I like to have these pre-mixed spice blends on hand in glass spice jars. I can just grab the one want to use that night and only have one jar out. It makes seasoning my meals quick and easy.

BBQ Seasoning
1. 1 teaspoon paprika
2. 1 teaspoon pepper
3. 1 teaspoon garlic powder
4. 1 teaspoon onion powder
5. ½ teaspoon salt
6. ½ teaspoon chili powder
7. ½ teaspoon cayenne pepper

Mexican Seasoning
1. 1 teaspoon garlic powder
2. 1 teaspoon onion powder
3. 1 teaspoon pepper
4. 1 teaspoon cumin
5. 1 teaspoon paprika
6. 1 teaspoon Creole seasoning

Italian Seasoning
1. 1 teaspoon garlic powder
2. 1 teaspoon onion powder
3. 1 teaspoon pepper
4. 3 teaspoons Italian herbs

BREAKFAST

Grapefruit and Almond Butter Rice Cakes

Ingredients:

1. 1 grapefruit
2. 2 large rice cakes
3. 2 tablespoons almond butter

Instructions:

1. Spread a tablespoon of almond butter on top of each rice cake.
2. Peel grapefruit.

Grapefruit & Yogurt

Ingredients:

1. 1 grapefruit
2. 1 cup plain Greek yogurt
3. 2 tablespoons vanilla protein powder

Instructions:

1. Peel grapefruit.
2. Stir protein powder into yogurt.

Strawberries & Yogurt

Ingredients:

1. 1 cup plain Greek yogurt
2. 2 tablespoons vanilla protein powder
3. 5 strawberries, sliced
4. 1 tablespoon walnuts, chopped

Instructions:

1. Mix protein powder into yogurt.
2. Add strawberries and walnuts and stir.

Blueberries & Yogurt

Ingredients:

1. 1 cup plain Greek yogurt
2. 1 tablespoon vanilla protein powder
3. ½ cup blueberries
4. 1 tablespoon sliced almonds

Instructions:

1. Mix protein powder into yogurt.
2. Add blueberries and almonds and stir.

Chocolate Yogurt

Ingredients:

1. 1 cup plain Greek yogurt
2. 2 tablespoons chocolate protein
3. 1 tablespoon almond butter

Instructions:

1. Mix all ingredients together and enjoy.

Eggs Benedict

Ingredients:

1. 2 eggs
2. 1 slice Ezekiel sprouted bread
3. 2 tablespoons plain Greek yogurt
4. 1 tablespoon brown mustard
5. ½ cup spinach
6. Pepper
7. Creole seasoning

Instructions:

1. Season eggs with pepper and Creole seasoning and cook to over easy.
2. Toast bread in toaster.
3. Mix yogurt and mustard in a small bowl.
4. Top bread with spinach and eggs, then pour sauce on top.

Pesto Eggs

Ingredients:

1. 2 eggs
2. ¼ cup diced peppers
3. ¼ cup fat free cheese
4. 1 teaspoon pesto
5. Salt
6. Pepper

Instructions:

1. Toss peppers in pan and spray with olive oil spray.
2. Cook on medium heat for 1 minute.
3. Crack eggs into pan.
4. Top with cheese, pesto, salt and pepper.
5. Stir and cook until done.

Veggie Omelet

Ingredients:

1. 1 cup egg whites
2. 1 cup spinach
3. ¼ cup diced sweet peppers
4. ¼ cup shredded fat-free cheddar cheese

Instructions:

1. Preheat skillet over medium heat and spray with non-stick spray.
2. Grill spinach and peppers.
3. Pour in egg whites and cook until firm.
4. Place cheese in the middle of the eggs.
5. Fold omelet over and eat!

Almond Butter Oatmeal

Ingredients:

1. ½ cup oats
2. 1 cup almond milk
3. 2 tablespoons almond butter
4. 1 tablespoon vanilla protein powder

Instructions:

1. Mix oats and almond milk. Microwave 1-2 minutes.
2. Stir remaining ingredients into cooked oatmeal.

Cinnamon Roll Oatmeal

Ingredients:

1. ½ cup oats
2. 1 cup almond milk
3. 1 tablespoon cinnamon
4. ¼ teaspoon vanilla
5. 1 tablespoon vanilla protein
6. 1 tablespoon cream cheese

Instructions:

1. Mix oats and almond milk. Microwave 1-2 minutes.
2. Stir other ingredients into cooked oatmeal.

Apple Cinnamon Oatmeal

Ingredients:

1. ½ cup oats
2. 1 cup almond milk
3. 1 apple, diced
4. 1 teaspoon cinnamon
5. 1 tablespoon vanilla protein powder
6. 1 tablespoon almonds, chopped

Instructions:

1. Mix apples, oats, and almond milk and microwave 1-2 minutes.

2. Stir all other ingredients into cooked oatmeal.

Chocolate Banana Oatmeal

Ingredients:

1. ½ cup oats
2. 1 cup almond milk
3. 1 banana, sliced
4. 1 teaspoon cocoa powder
5. 1 tablespoon. vanilla protein powder

Instructions:

1. Mix oats and almond milk. Microwave 1-2 minutes.
2. Add remaining ingredients to cooked oatmeal and stir.

Banana Shake

Ingredients:

1. 1 banana
2. 1 scoop vanilla protein
3. 1 cup spinach
4. 2 tablespoons almond butter
5. Ice

Instructions:

1. Blend all ingredients in a blender until smooth.

Blueberry Shake

Ingredients:

1. ½ cup blueberries
2. 1 cup spinach
3. 8 ounces unsweetened, vanilla almond milk
4. 1 scoop vanilla protein powder
5. Ice

Instructions:

1. Blend all ingredients together in a blender until smooth.

Strawberry Shake

Ingredients:

1. ½ cup strawberries
2. 1 cup spinach
3. 8 ounces unsweetened, vanilla almond milk
4. 1 scoop vanilla protein powder
5. Ice

Instructions:

1. Blend all ingredients together in a blender until smooth.

Breakfast Sandwich

Ingredients:

1. 1 slice Ezekiel bread
2. ½ cup spinach
3. 2 Slices turkey bacon
4. 2 eggs
5. 2 tablespoons pico
6. Olive oil spray

Instructions:

1. Spray pan with olive oil spray and heat to medium heat.
2. Cook turkey bacon until crisp and set to side.
3. Cook eggs until firm enough to flip. Flip and turn burner off.
4. Toast bread in toaster until warm.
5. Top bread with spinach, eggs, turkey bacon, and pico.

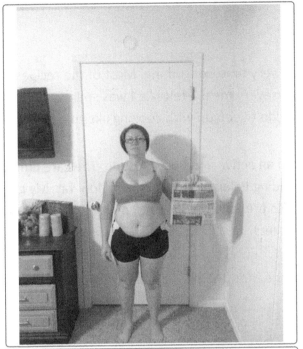

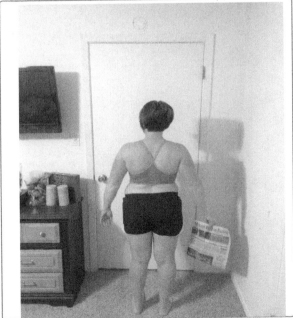
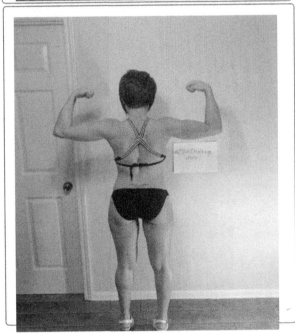

THE PROBLEM

Paleo recipes are delicious, but they tend to be very time-consuming. Most of the recipes involve chopping vegetables and using multiple pans at every meal. I felt like I was spending all my time in the kitchen. When I went back to work, I couldn't keep up with cooking like that anymore.

I adapted the recipes in this cookbook to fit into an active and busy lifestyle. They are pulled from my past four years of eating various diets, including Paleo, gluten-free, and low-fat. My goal with these recipes is to have your snacks and lunches prepped on Sundays in less than one hour, and for all your dinners to be done in 30 minutes or less.

Healthy eating should be accessible for everyone, not just the select few who have the time to cook gourmet meals!

Fiesta Eggs

Ingredients:

1. 1 egg
2. ½ cup egg whites
3. ½ cup spinach
4. 2 tablespoons Pico
5. ¼ cup fat-free cheese of choice
6. Pepper
7. Creole seasoning

Instructions:

1. Preheat skillet to medium.
2. Grill Pico and spinach for 2 minutes.
3. Pour in egg, egg whites, and cheese and stir.
4. Season with pepper and Creole seasoning.
5. Keep stirring for fluffy eggs until cooked.

Breakfast Quesadilla

Ingredients:

1. 1 egg
2. ¼ cup egg whites
3. ¼ cup diced peppers
4. 1 tablespoon Pico
5. 1 cup spinach, torn up
6. ¼ cup fat-free cheese
7. 1 Ezekiel tortilla

Instructions:

1. Cook spinach, Pico, and diced peppers until slightly softened.
2. Pour in egg and egg whites.
3. Stir often until eggs are done.
4. Place half of cheese on half of tortilla and top with egg mixture.
5. Place other half of cheese on top of eggs and fold tortilla in half.
6. Heat in skillet on each side until cheese is melted.
7. Remove from pan, cut into 4 slices with a pizza cutter.

Strawberry French Toast

Ingredients:

1. 2 slices Ezekiel bread
2. ½ cup egg whites
3. ¼ cup Unsweetened, vanilla almond milk
4. 1 teaspoon cinnamon
5. 2 tablespoons almond butter
6. 6 strawberries, sliced

Instructions:

1. Whisk cinnamon and almond milk into egg whites.
2. Put 2 slices of bread into the mixture to soak.
3. Put bread in pan and pour remaining egg whites onto bread.
4. Cook bread slices on medium heat for about 4 minutes on each side, until eggs are cooked.
5. Spread almond butter on each slice of bread.
6. Place strawberries on one slice of bread and top with the other slice to make a sandwich.

Banana French Toast

Ingredients:

1. 2 slices Ezekiel bread
2. ½ cup egg whites
3. ¼ cup unsweetened, vanilla almond milk
4. 1 teaspoon cinnamon
5. 2 tablespoons almond butter
6. 1 Small banana, sliced

Instructions:

1. Whisk cinnamon and almond milk into egg whites.
2. Put 2 slices of bread into the mixture to soak.
3. Put bread in pan and pour remaining egg whites onto bread.
4. Cook bread slices on medium heat for about 4 minutes on each side until eggs are cooked.
5. Spread almond butter on each slice of bread.
6. Place banana on one slice of bread and top with the other slice to make a sandwich.

SNACKS

Hard Boiled Eggs
>   2 hardboiled eggs

Cucumber
>   1 cucumber sliced
>   pepper

Veggies & Hummus

>   Unlimited raw veggies

>   ¼ cup hummus

Veggies & Guacamole

>   Unlimited raw veggies

>   1 Wholly Guacamole Mini Pack

Nut Thins & Guacamole

>   1 serving Nut Thins

>   1 Wholly Guacamole Mini Pack

Nut Thins & Hummus

>   1 serving Nut Thins

>   ¼ cup hummus

Turkey & Nut Thins

>   6 slices of turkey

>   1 serving of Nut Thins

Apple and Almond Butter

1 apple

2 tablespoons almond butter

Banana & Almond Butter

Banana

2 tablespoons almond butter

Turkey & Cheese

3-6 slices turkey

1 mozzarella string cheese

Apple & Almonds

1 apple

2 servings almonds

Tuna & Rice Cake

1 packet of tuna

1 rice cake

Rice Cakes

2 rice cakes

2 tablespoons almond butter

Smoked Salmon

2 slices smoked salmon

1 mozzarella String cheese

Yogurt & Fruit

     1 cup plain Greek yogurt

     ½ cup fruit

Pineapple and Cottage Cheese

     1 cup cottage cheese

     ½ cup pineapple

Sweet Potato

     sweet potato

LUNCHES

Tuna Spinach Salad

Ingredients:

1.   1 large tuna packet
2.   2 cups spinach
3.   ¼ cup chopped almonds
4.   ½ an avocado, diced

Instructions:

1. Place spinach in container.
2. Top spinach with all other ingredients and enjoy.

Spicy Tuna Wrap

Ingredients:

1. 1 package tuna
2. 1 tablespoon Sriracha
3. ½ teaspoon liquid aminos
4. 1 cup spinach
5. ½ avocado, diced
6. 1 sprouted tortilla

Instructions:

1. Open tuna packet and dump contents into your container.
2. Top with liquid aminos and sriracha.
3. Place spinach next to the tuna.
4. Cut an avocado in half and remove the seed.
5. Dice the avocado while still in the skin and place it face down on top of the spinach.
6. Put tortilla in a sandwich bag.
7. On the day of, top your tortilla with the tuna and spinach.
8. Spoon the avocado out of the skin and put it on top of the filled tortilla.
9. Roll tortilla into a burrito and eat.

Salmon Spinach Salad

Ingredients:

1. 1 salmon packet
2. 2 cups spinach
3. ¼ cup chopped almonds
4. ½ avocado-diced

Instructions:

1. Place spinach in container.
2. Top spinach with all other ingredients and enjoy.

Turkey Wrap

Ingredients:

1. 6 slices of turkey
2. ½ avocado
3. 1 cup spinach and lettuce mix
4. 1 Ezekiel sprouted tortilla
5. Pepper
6. Dijon mustard (optional)

Instructions:

1. Spread mustard onto tortilla if using.
2. Layer turkey onto tortilla.
3. Top with all other ingredients and roll up into a wrap.

Buffalo Chicken Wrap

Ingredients:

1. 1 can (5 ounces) chicken
2. 1 cup spinach
3. 1 Ezekiel sprouted tortilla
4. 1 tablespoon hot wing sauce

Instructions:

1. Drain chicken and place in your container.
2. Place wing sauce on chicken.
3. Put spinach next to chicken in your container.
4. Put tortilla in a sandwich bag.
5. On the day of, put ingredients in burrito and enjoy.

Quesadilla

Ingredients:

1. 1 can (5 ounces) chicken
2. 1 Ezekiel sprouted tortilla
3. 2 tablespoons Pico
4. ½ cup low-fat shredded cheese
5. Mexican seasoning

Instructions:

1. Drain chicken and season with Mexican seasoning.
2. Put tortilla in pan and top half of tortilla with half of the shredded cheese.
3. Top cheese with chicken and Pico.
4. Put other half of cheese on top of chicken.
5. Fold tortilla in half.
6. Grill for 5 minutes on each side to melt cheese.
7. Cut into 3 pieces and put in container for lunch.

Mexican Burrito

Ingredients:

1. 1 can (5 ounces) chicken
2. ½ avocado, diced
3. 1 cup spinach
4. 1 Ezekiel sprouted tortilla
5. 2 tablespoons pico or salsa

Instructions:

1. Open chicken and put in your container, top with pico.
2. Dice avocado in shell and place upside-down in your container
3. Place spinach in container.
4. Put tortilla in a sandwich bag.
5. On the day of, load tortilla with toppings and enjoy.

Chicken Salad

Ingredients:

1. 1 can (5 ounces) chicken
2. 2 cups spinach leaves
3. 12 almonds
4. ½ avocado (diced)
5. Pepper
6. 1 tablespoon Bragg's liquid aminos, or balsamic vinegar

Instructions:

1. Place spinach in container.
2. Top with canned chicken, almonds, avocado, and pepper.
3. On the day of, add dressing just before eating.
4. Place lid on container and shake it up, then enjoy.

Black Bean Burger

Ingredients:

1. 2 black bean veggie burgers
2. ½ avocado
3. ¼ cup fat-free mozzarella cheese
4. 1 slice Ezekiel sprouted bread
5. 1 tablespoon Pico
6. ¼ cup lettuce or spinach

Instructions:

1. Place burgers in container and top with mozzarella cheese.
2. Place spinach and Pico beside burger and the slice of bread in a sandwich bag.
3. Cut avocado in half, remove pit, then cut slices in the avocado while still in the skin. Put half of the avocado face down on the spinach and Pico in your container.
4. On the day of, microwave the burgers with the cheese on top, until warm and cheese is melted.
5. Use a spoon to scoop the avocado slices out of the skin.
6. Serve on top of bread, then top with lettuce, avocado, and Pico.

Pizza Burger

Ingredients:

1. 1 slice Ezekiel sprouted bread
2. 2 black bean veggie burgers
3. 3 tablespoons marinara sauce
4. Turkey pepperoni
5. ¼ cup fat-free mozzarella cheese

Instructions:

1. Place slice of bread in a sandwich bag.
2. Place burgers in your container along with the turkey pepperoni and cheese.
3. Place marinara sauce in a leak-proof container.
4. On the day of, lay burgers on a plate.
5. Top burgers with marinara, turkey pepperoni, and cheese.
6. Microwave until warm and cheese is melted.
7. Place burgers on top of bread and enjoy.

Pizza Wrap

Ingredients:

1. 1 sprouted tortilla
2. ¼ cup marinara sauce
3. ½ cup fat-free mozzarella cheese
4. ½ package turkey pepperoni

Instructions:

1. Place pepperoni and cheese in your container.
2. Pour marinara sauce on top of the pepperoni.
3. Place tortilla in a sandwich bag.
4. On the day of, top the tortilla with the pepperoni mixture, roll it up and enjoy.

Chicken & Broccoli

Ingredients:

1. 1 can (5 ounces) chicken
2. 1-2 cups broccoli (steamable or make your own)
3. 1 tablespoon liquid aminos

Instructions:

1. Drain chicken and put into your container.
2. Put broccoli in a sandwich bag, stab with a fork a few times, and add to your container.
3. Pour liquid aminos into a small leak-proof container.
4. On the day of, pour liquid aminos on top of chicken and microwave all for 1 minute to warm up chicken and steam your broccoli.

Chicken & Green Beans

Ingredients:

1. 1 can (5 ounces) chicken
2. 1-2 cups green beans
3. ½ cup black beans
4. Pepper
5. Garlic powder
6. Creole seasoning

Instructions:

1. Drain chicken and put into your container.
2. Put green beans in a sandwich bag, season with garlic powder and pepper, stab with a fork a few times, and add to your container.
3. Spoon black beans into container.
4. Season chicken with pepper and Creole seasoning.

Chicken & Broccoli

Ingredients:

1. 1 can (5 ounces) chicken
2. 1-2 cups broccoli
3. ½ cup black beans
4. Pepper
5. Garlic powder
6. Creole seasoning

Instructions:

1. Drain chicken and put into your container.
2. Put broccoli in a sandwich bag and season with garlic powder, pepper, and Creole seasoning. Stab with a fork a few times and add to your container.
3. Spoon black beans into container.
4. Season chicken with pepper and Creole seasoning.

Tuna & Rice Cakes

Ingredients:

1. 2 packets (5 ounces each) of tuna
2. 2 rice cakes
3. 1 avocado
4. Pepper
5. 1 bag steamable veggies

Instructions:

1. Place rice cakes in your container.
2. Cut avocado in half, remove pit, then cut slices into the avocado while still in the skin. Put one half in the container next to your rice cakes, face down.
3. Put 1-2 cups of veggies in a sandwich bag and stab holes in it. Place in container if room or leave separate.
4. On the day of, microwave your veggies for 30-60 seconds.
5. Put tuna on top of rice cakes and sprinkle with pepper.
6. Use a spoon to scoop the avocado slices out of the skin and put on top of your tuna.
7. Serve with veggies and enjoy.

Blueberry Salad

Ingredients:

1. 1 can (5 ounces) chicken
2. 1 cup lettuce
3. 1 cup spinach
4. ¼ cup blueberries (I use frozen)
5. 1 tablespoon almond, chopped
6. 1 tablespoon Bragg's liquid aminos, or 2 tablespoons balsamic vinegar

Instructions:

1. Place spinach and lettuce in your container.
2. Open chicken and place on top of lettuce.
3. Top with blueberries and almonds.
4. Place dressing of choice in a small, leak-proof container.
5. On the day of, top with dressing and enjoy.

Turkey Sandwich

Ingredients:

1. 2 slices Ezekiel bread
2. 6-8 slices of turkey
3. 1 avocado, mashed or sliced
4. 1 tablespoon Dijon mustard
5. Pepper

Instructions:

1. Place bread in a sandwich bag.
2. Cut avocado in half and remove pit. Slice avocado while in the skin and place pit back in middle.
3. Put full avocado in the container. Add turkey slices to container.
4. Place Dijon mustard in a small, leak-proof container.
5. On the day of, scoop the avocado slices out and place on the bread.
6. Top the avocado with the turkey.
7. Spread Dijon mustard on other slice of bread and sprinkle with pepper.

Salmon Sandwich

Ingredients:

1. 1 packet of salmon (5 ounces)
2. 1 avocado
3. 1 tablespoon salsa or Pico
4. ½ cup spinach
5. 1 slice Ezekiel bread

Instructions:

1. Place bread in a sandwich bag and place in your container.
2. Cut avocado in half and remove pit. Slice avocado while in the skin and place pit back in middle.
3. Put full avocado in the container.
4. Put spinach in your container.
5. Spoon Pico or salsa into small, leak-proof container.
6. On the day of, top bread with spinach, Pico or salsa, and contents of salmon packet.
7. Use a spoon to scoop the sliced avocado out of the skin and top your sandwich with it.

Tuna Sandwich

Ingredients:

1. 1 packet of tuna (6 ounces)
2. 2 tablespoons Greek yogurt
3. 1 teaspoon hot mustard
4. 2 tablespoons chopped walnuts
5. ½ cup spinach
6. 1 slice Ezekiel sprouted bread

Instructions:

1. Mix tuna with yogurt, hot mustard, and walnuts.
2. Spoon into container.
3. Place spinach next to tuna.
4. Put bread in a sandwich bag.
5. On the day of, top the bread with the spinach and spoon tuna mixture onto it.

Pesto Turkey Sandwich

Ingredients:

1. 3 slices turkey meat
2. 1 tablespoon pesto
3. 1 cup spinach
4. 2 slices Ezekiel sprouted bread
5. 1 slice low-Fat cheese
6. ½ avocado, sliced

Instructions:

1. Place turkey, cheese and spinach in your container.
2. Top turkey with pesto.
3. Place sliced avocado upside down on top of the spinach.
4. Put bread in a sandwich bag.
5. On the day of, put all ingredients in the bread and enjoy.

Chicken Caesar Wrap

Ingredients:

1. 1 can (5 ounces) chicken
2. 1 cup spinach
3. 2 tablespoons Caesar dressing
4. ¼ cup grated parmesan cheese
5. 1 Ezekiel sprouted tortilla

Instructions:

1. Open chicken and spoon into your container.
2. Place spinach next to chicken and top with cheese.
3. Put Caesar dressing in a leak proof container.
4. Put tortilla in a large storage bag.
5. On the day of, pour dressing into container and stir.
6. Use quarters of tortillas and top with mixture to eat.

Buffalo Chicken Wrap

Ingredients:

1. 1 can (5 ounces) chicken
2. 1 cup spinach
3. 2 tablespoons buffalo sauce
4. ¼ cup grated mozzarella cheese
5. **1 Ezekiel sprouted tortilla**

Instructions:

1. Open chicken and spoon into your container.
2. Place spinach next to chicken and top with cheese.
3. Pour wing sauce on the chicken.
4. Put tortilla in a large storage bag.
5. On the day of stir all ingredients.
6. Use quarters of tortillas and top with mixture to eat.

Sriracha Chicken Wrap

Ingredients:

1. 1 can (5 ounces) chicken
2. 1 cup spinach
3. 1 tablespoon Sriracha sauce
4. ¼ cup grated mozzarella cheese
5. 1 Ezekiel sprouted tortilla

Instructions:

1. Open chicken and spoon into your container.
2. Place spinach next to chicken and top with cheese.
3. Pour Sriracha sauce on the chicken.
4. Put tortilla in a large storage bag.
5. On the day of, stir all ingredients.
6. On the day of, wrap mixture in tortilla and enjoy.

DINNERS

Lemon Pepper Chicken

Ingredients:

1. 1 chicken breast
2. 1 lemon
3. ½ cup black beans
4. 1 cup broccoli
5. Lemon pepper seasoning

Instructions:

1. Heat skillet over medium heat.
2. Season chicken with the juice of 1 lemon and the lemon pepper.
3. Steam broccoli in microwave or pan.
4. Cook chicken in skillet until no longer pink inside.
5. Heat beans in skillet next to chicken.
6. Serve warm.

Family Friendly Tip:

My kids will eat this meal. I usually add a side the younger children will eat like macaroni and cheese.

Extra Ingredients:

1. Macaroni & Cheese

Chicken & Brussel Sprouts

Ingredients:

1. 1 tablespoon minced garlic
2. 1 chicken breast
3. Mrs. Dash Garlic and Herb seasoning
4. 1 cup Brussels sprouts
5. 1 tablespoon balsamic vinegar
6. Garlic powder
7. Pepper
8. 1 tablespoon olive oil

Instructions:

1. Wash brussels sprouts, cut ends off, and cut in half.
2. Throw sprouts in a bowl and add olive oil, balsamic vinegar, garlic powder, and pepper.
3. Spread on a cookie sheet covered with foil and bake at 350° for about 15 minutes.
4. Coat chicken with garlic and garlic and herb seasoning.
5. Cook on medium heat until no longer pink inside.

Family Friendly Tip:

My kids will eat this meal. I usually add a side the younger children will eat like jasmine rice.

Extra Ingredients:

1. Jasmine Rice

Balsamic Chicken

Ingredients:

1. 1 tablespoon balsamic vinegar
2. 1 chicken breast
3. Ilalian seasoning
4. 1/2 box cherry tomatoes
5. 1/2 bunch asparagus
6. 1 tsp olive oil

Instructions:

1. Heat skillet over medium heat.
2. Season chicken with Italian seasoning and pour balsamic vinegar on it.
3. Cook on medium heat until no longer pink.
4. Slice tomatoes in half and put in a separate pan on medium heat with 1 tsp olive oil.
5. Remove bottom half of asparagus and place in pan with tomatoes.
6. Season vegetables with Italian seasoning and cook until slightly softened.

Family Friendly Tip:

My kids will eat this meal. I usually add a side of pasta and tomato sauce.

Extra Ingredients:

1. Pasta & tomato sauce

Grilled Salmon

Ingredients:

1. 4 ounces salmon
2. 1 cup green beans
3. 1 tablespoon coconut oil
4. Cajun seasoning

Instructions:

1. Heat skillet over medium heat and add coconut oil.
2. Cook green beans in steam bag or on stove.
3. Season salmon with Cajun seasoning and cook until crispy on the outside and the filet flakes apart when stabbed with a fork.

Family Friendly Tip:

My kids will not eat anything in this meal! When I make this, I usually let them eat junk that night.

Extra Ingredients:

1. Corn dogs or Totinos pizza rolls

Salmon with Garlic Aioli Sauce

Ingredients:

1. 4 ounces salmon
2. 1 cup green beans
3. 1 tablespoon plain Greek yogurt
4. 1 tablespoon brown mustard
5. ¼ teaspoon garlic
6. Pepper
7. Creole seasoning

Instructions:

1. Cook salmon over medium heat for approximately 4 minutes on each side, until salmon pulls apart easily with a fork.
2. Steam green beans in microwave, and season with Creole seasoning and pepper.
3. In a small bowl, stir garlic, Greek yogurt. and brown mustard together.
4. After you flip the salmon, top with the sauce.

Family Friendly Tip:

My kids will not eat anything in this meal. I let them eat junk this night.

Extra ingredients:

1. Corn dogs or Totinos pizza rolls

Turkey Burger

Ingredients:

1. 1 sweet potato
2. 1 lean turkey burger
3. 1 slice Ezekiel sprouted bread
4. 1 avocado
5. ½ cup of lettuce
6. 2 tablespoons fat-free mozzarella cheese
7. Pepper

Instructions:

1. Score sweet potato and cook in microwave (with potato bag) for 4 minutes.
2. Season turkey burger with pepper.
3. Preheat skillet to medium and cook turkey burger until middle is warm.
4. Place turkey burger on top of bread slice, and top with mozzarella, avocado, and lettuce.
5. Serve with plain sweet potato.

Family Friendly Tip:

My kids will eat this meal. I usually add a side like chips, tater tots, or French fries.

Extra Ingredients:

1. Tator-tots or French fries

Mexican Chicken

Ingredients:

1. 1 chicken breast
2. 2 tablespoons Pico
3. ¼ cup diced bell peppers
4. ½ avocado
5. ½ cup black beans
6. Mexican seasoning

Instructions:

1. Preheat skillet over medium heat.
2. Season chicken with Mexican seasoning.
3. Cook chicken for about 5 minutes on each side, placing peppers and Pico in the pan once the chicken is done.
4. When the veggies have softened, add black beans to the pan until warm.

Family Friendly Tip:

My kids will eat this meal without the toppings on the chicken, so I remove their chicken from the pan before I add the peppers and Pico. I usually add a side the younger children will eat like brown rice and ranch-style beans.

Extra Ingredients:

1. Brown rice cups
2. Ranch-style beans

BBQ Chicken

Ingredients:

1.   1 chicken breast
2.   2 tablespoons sugar-free BBQ sauce
3.   1 sweet potato
4.   BBQ seasoning

Instructions:

1. Heat skillet over medium heat.
2. Season chicken with BBQ seasoning.
3. Cook chicken in pan until no longer pink.
4. While chicken is cooking, score sweet potato and microwave in potato cooker for 4 minutes.

Family Friendly Tip:

My kids will eat this meal without the BBQ sauce, so I put the BBQ sauce on after I put our chicken on our plates. I usually add a side the kids will eat like brown rice and ranch-style beans.

Extra Ingredients:

1. Brown rice cups
2. Ranch-style beans.

Spaghetti Squash

Ingredients:

1. 1 spaghetti squash
2. 1 cup spaghetti sauce
3. Italian herb seasoning

Instructions:

1. Preheat oven to 400°F.
2. Wash and stab spaghetti squash with a fork several times.
3. Microwave squash for 5 minutes, turning several times.
4. Slice spaghetti squash in half and scoop all seeds out with a spoon.
5. Cover a cookie sheet with foil and spray with olive oil spray.
6. Place squash on cookie sheet face down and bake squash for 30 minutes or until it is easily stabbed with a fork.
7. Warm spaghetti sauce in your serving bowl in the microwave for 1 minute.
8. Season sauce with Italian herb seasoning.
9. Remove squash from oven and turn over. Use a fork to shred the squash into spaghetti-like strings.
10. Add squash to your sauce and enjoy.

Family Friendly Tip:

My kids will eat this as regular spaghetti, so I make them spaghetti noodles and meatballs.

Extra Ingredients:

1. Spaghetti pasta
2. Large bag of frozen meatballs
3. More spaghetti sauce

**This is a weekend meal.

Spaghetti

Ingredients:

1. 1 box zucchini noodles
2. 1 cup spaghetti sauce
3. Italian herb seasoning
4. 1 Tbsp Olive Oil

Instructions:

1. Pour olive oil in a skillet and heat on medium.
2. Toss zucchini noodles into the oil and season with Italian herb seasoning.
3. Cook on medium heat until slightly softened.

Family Friendly Tip:

My kids will eat this as regular spaghetti, so I make them spaghetti noodles and meatballs.

Extra Ingredients:

1. Spaghetti pasta
2. Large bag of frozen meatballs
3. More spaghetti sauce

Cajun Fish

Ingredients:

1. 1 wild-caught white fish fillet (I usually get flounder)
2. Mrs. Dash Cajun seasoning (or Mexican seasoning)
3. 2 tablespoons salsa
4. ½ cup brown rice
5. ½ avocado
6. ½ cup green beans
7. Garlic powder 8. Pepper
9. Olive oil spray

Instructions:

1. Spray pan with olive oil spray and heat to medium.
2. Season fish fillet and cook until flakey.
3. Warm rice in microwave.
4. Steam green beans in a plastic bag for 30 seconds and season with garlic powder and pepper.
5. Pour rice on plate and top with fish, salsa, and avocado.
6. Serve green beans on the side.

Family Friendly Tip:

My kids will eat this meal without the toppings on the fish. I make them extra rice to go with it.

Extra Ingredients:

1. White rice

Mango Fish

Ingredients:

1. 1 wild-caught white fish fillet
2. 2 tablespoons mango salsa
3. 1 cup green beans
4. ½ cup brown rice
5. Creole seasoning

Instructions:

1. Season fish and grill for 2-3 minutes on each side.
2. Steam green beans until softened. Season with Creole seasoning.
3. Warm brown rice for 1 minute in the microwave.
4. Top fish with mango salsa and serve with rice and green beans.

Family Friendly Tip:

My kids will eat this meal without the toppings on the fish. I make them extra rice to go with it.

Extra Ingredients:

1. White rice

Stuffed Bell Peppers

Ingredients:

1. 1½ cups ground turkey
2. ¼ cup mushrooms, chopped
3. 2 tablespoons Pico
4. Mexican seasoning
5. ¼ cup fat-free shredded cheese
6. 2 green bell peppers, top and seeds removed
7. ½ cup rice

Instructions:

1. Preheat oven to 350°F.
2. Season turkey generously with Mexican seasoning and cook until browned.
3. Add chopped mushrooms and Pico to the ground turkey and cook another 2 minutes.
4. Place bell peppers on a covered cookie sheet.
5. Warm rice in microwave.
6. Put half of the rice and half of the ground turkey mixture in each bell pepper.
7. Top with cheese.
8. Cook in oven for 10 minutes.

Family Tip:

My kids won't eat the veggies here, so I remove the ground turkey for them before I add the mushrooms and Pico. I make extra rice and serve them burritos with rice.

Extra Ingredients:

1. Flour tortillas
2. Brown rice

Shrimp Lettuce Wraps

Ingredients:

1. 1 cup peeled and deveined shrimp
2. 6 tablespoons liquid aminos, split
3. 1 tablespoon olive oil
4. Cauliflower rice mix
5. 1 bag broccoli slaw
6. 1 tablespoon Dijon mustard
7. ¼ cup Greek yogurt
8. Romain lettuce leaf

Instructions:

1. Cook shrimp over medium heat. Once thawed, drain water from pan and add liquid aminos. Cook until pink.
2. In a separate pan, heat olive oil and add the cauliflower rice mix and 2 tablespoons of the liquid aminos. Stir often and cook until hot.
3. Mix broccoli slaw, Dijon mustard, Greek yogurt, and 3 tablespoons of the liquid aminos in a bowl.
4. Top lettuce leaves with shrimp and broccoli slaw.
5. Serve with cauliflower rice.

Family Tip:

Some of my kids love shrimp, so I add brown rice or make burritos with the shrimp without the broccoli slaw. The ones who don't like shrimp get hot dogs!

Extra Ingredients:

1. Tortillas
2. Brown rice
3. Hot dogs

Pesto Chicken

Ingredients:

1. 1 chicken breast
2. 2 tablespoons pesto
3. Italian seasoning
4. 1-2 cups mixed lettuce
5. 1 tablespoon Italian dressing

Instructions:

1. Season chicken with Italian seasoning and grill over medium heat for 3-4 minutes per side.
2. Brush pesto onto chicken with a spoon.
3. Put lettuce on your plate and top with Italian dressing.
4. Serve with chicken.

Family Friendly Tip:

My kids will eat this meal without the toppings on the chicken. I make them rice to go with it.

Extra Ingredients:

1. White rice

Mexican Burrito Bowl

Ingredients:

1. 1 chicken breast, diced
2. ½ cup brown rice
3. 1 cup black beans
4. ½ cup sweet peppers, diced
5. 2 tablespoons Pico
6. ½ avocado, diced
7. Mexican seasoning
8. 1 teaspoon olive oil
9. 1 tablespoon salsa

Instructions:

1. Heat olive oil over medium heat.
2. Add Pico and diced peppers and stir.
3. Season chicken with Mexican seasoning and add to pan.
4. Add black beans and rice to pan when chicken is done.
5. Pour into a bowl.
6. Top with diced avocado and salsa.

Family Friendly Tip:

My kids will eat this chicken. I make them burritos out of the chicken and serve the beans on the side.

Extra Ingredients:

1. Flour tortillas

Turkey Burrito Bowl

Ingredients:

1. ¼ pound ground turkey
2. ½ cup brown rice
3. 1 cup black beans
4. ½ cup sweet peppers, diced
5. 2 tablespoons Pico
6. ½ avocado, diced
7. Mexican seasoning
8. 1 teaspoon olive oil
9. 1 tablespoon salsa or Pico

Instructions:

1. Heat olive oil over medium heat.
2. Add Pico and diced peppers and stir.
3. Season turkey with Mexican seasoning and add to pan. Stir often until cooked.
4. Add black beans and rice to pan and cook until warm.
5. Pour the mixture into a bowl. Top with diced avocado and salsa.

Family Friendly Tip:

My kids will eat this as burritos. I serve their beans on the side.

Extra Ingredients:

1. Flour tortillas

Chili

Ingredients:

1. ¼ pound ground turkey
2. 1 tablespoon garlic
3. ¼ cup diced sweet peppers
4. ½ can tomato sauce
5. 1 tablespoon Pico
6. 1 tablespoon coconut aminos
7. 1 tablespoon Mexican seasoning
8. 1 teaspoon olive oil, divided
9. Zucchini noodles

Instructions:

1. Heat half of the olive oil in pan over medium heat.
2. Add diced sweet peppers and stir for 1 minute.
3. Add garlic, Pico, and coconut aminos and stir.
4. Add turkey and season with Mexican seasoning. Cook until done.
5. Pour tomato sauce on meat and heat until warm.
6. Heat other the half of the olive oil in a second pan.
7. Add zucchini noodles to second pan and stir.
8. Cook zucchini noodles until a bit soft, approximately 2 minutes.
9. Put noodles in a bowl and top with meat mixture.

Family Friendly Tip:

My kids don't like homemade chili, so I usually buy them canned chili and serve it with hot dogs or Fritos.

Extra Ingredients:

1. Canned chili
2. Hot dogs

Zucchini Boats

Ingredients:

1. 1 cup ground turkey
2. Mexican seasoning
3. 2 tablespoons marinara
4. 2 zucchinis
5. ¼ cup fat-free mozzarella

Instructions:

1. Preheat oven to 350°F.
2. Cut tips off the zucchinis and then cut them in half longways.
3. Spoon the seeds out of the zucchini.
4. Line a cookie sheet and place the zucchini halves in the oven on 350°F for 5 minutes.
5. Season ground turkey with Mexican seasoning and cook it in a pan on the stove until browned.
6. Mix marinara in meat when finished.
7. Remove pan from the oven, spoon meat mixture into zucchini, and top with mozzarella.
8. Place back in oven and cook until cheese is melted.

Family Friendly Tip:

My kids love this meat in burritos. I will make extra ground turkey and ranch-style beans for them.

Extra Ingredients:

1. Flour tortillas
2. Ranch-style beans

Pizza Zucchini Boats

Ingredients:

1. ½ cup turkey pepperoni
2. Italian seasoning
3. 2 tablespoons marinara sauce
4. 2 Zucchini
5. ¼ cup fat-free mozzarella

Instructions:

1. Preheat oven to Cut tips off the zucchinis and then cut them in half longways.
2. Spoon the seeds out of the zucchini.
3. Line a cookie sheet, place zucchini halves on it, and place in oven on 350°F for 5 minutes.
4. Season turkey pepperoni with Italian seasoning.
5. Mix turkey and marinara in a bowl.
6. Remove pan from the oven, spoon pepperoni mixture into zucchini, and top with mozzarella.
7. Place pan back in the oven and cook until cheese is melted.

Family Friendly Tip:

I will make little pizzas on tortillas when I make this. Just spoon some marinara on the tortilla. Top with the turkey pepperoni and mozzarella and bake for about 5 minutes.

Extra Ingredients:

1. Flour tortillas

Pho Soup

Ingredients:

1. 2 boiled eggs, sliced in half
2. 2 cups vegetable broth
3. 2 tablespoons garlic
4. 1 jalapeño, chopped
5. 1 scallion, chopped
6. ¼ teaspoon onion powder
7. ¼ teaspoon pepper
8. Zucchini noodles

Instructions:

1. Pour broth into pan and heat on medium heat.
2. Season broth with onion powder and pepper.
3. Add garlic, boiled eggs, and zucchini noodles and bring to a boil.
4. Boil for 4 minutes to soften noodles.
5. Pour into bowl and top with chopped jalapeño and scallion to taste.

Family Friendly Tip:

My kids won't eat this at all. They usually eat corn dogs or Totino's Pizza Rolls when I make this.

Extra Ingredients:

1. Corn dogs or Totinos pizza rolls

Made in the USA
Middletown, DE
06 December 2024

66303578R00044

9181853R0

Made in the USA
Charleston, SC
17 August 2011